The Complete Guitar Player Songbook 3

**Use with
The Complete Guitar Player course
or on its own!**

This songbook is designed to complement
The Complete Guitar Player Book 3, presenting the songs
from the book with full melodic lines and lyrics.
In addition to the songs featured in the series, this book
contains some suitable additional songs to help
you develop your technique and expand your repertoire.

Sometimes, capo and tuning indications are shown.
This is so that you can play along with the original recording
in the right key. If you're playing on your own,
you don't need to worry about these instructions.

HAL•LEONARD®

Published by
Hal Leonard

Exclusive distributors:

Hal Leonard
7777 West Bluemound Road,
Milwaukee, WI 53213
Email: info@halleonard.com

Hal Leonard Europe Limited
42 Wigmore Street Maryleborne,
London, WIU 2 RN
Email: info@halleonardeurope.com

Hal Leonard Australia Pty. Ltd.
4 Lentara Court Cheltenham,
Victoria, 9132 Australia
Email: info@halleonard.com.au

Order No.AM995434
ISBN 978-1-84772-734-3
This book © Copyright 2014 Hal Leonard

Edited by Toby Knowles.
Music arranged by Matt Cowe.
Music processed by Paul Ewers Music Design.
Cover designed by Michael Bell Design.
All photographs courtesy of Getty Images:
Bob Dylan, The Hollies, Paul Simon, Cat Stevens by Michael Ochs Archives.
The Beatles by Mark & Colleen Hayward/Redferns.
Leonard Cohen by Rob Verhorst/Redferns.
Noel Gallagher by Mick Hutson/Redferns. Oasis by Michel Linssen/Redferns.
Elvis Presley by Alan Band/Keystone / Simon & Garfunkel by Gilles Petard.

Printed in EU.

www.halleonard.com

The First Cut Is The Deepest

Words & Music by Cat Stevens

Arpeggio style:

Try to memorise the chord sequence. That way, you can concentrate on the sound, rather than reading, when you play this song.

try_____ to love a - gain.
try_____ to love a - gain.

Ba - by, I'll try_____

_____ to love a - gain but I know_____

Chorus

The first cut is the deep - est ba - by I know_____ the first cut is the deep-

- est.   'Cause when it comes to be - in' luck - y she's cursed,_____

_____   when it comes to lov - in' me she's worse._____   But when it

comes to be - ing loved she's_____ first,_____   that's how I know:_____

The first cut is the deep - est ba - by I know_

Hallelujah

Words & Music by Leonard Cohen

Arpeggio style:

Focus on playing the picking pattern as precisely as possible. Let the notes of the chord ring out—this will really help the music flow.

Accompaniment: 6/8 Rhythm
Capo: Fret 5

Intro

Verse

(1.) heard there was a se-cret chord that Da - vid played and it pleased the Lord, but
(2.) faith was strong but you need-ed proof. You saw her bath-ing on the roof, her

(Verses 3, 4 & 6 see block lyrics)

(Verses 5 Instrumental)

you don't real - ly care for mu - sic do ya? Well, it
beau - ty and the moon - light ov - er - threw ya. And she

7

Verse 3:
Well, baby I've been here before
I've seen this room, and I've walked this floor,
You know, I used to live alone before I knew you
And I've seen your flag on the marble arch
And love is not a victory march
It's a cold and it's a broken Hallelujah

Verse 4:
Well, there was a time when you let me know
What's really going on below
But now you never show that to me do ya?
But remember when I moved in you
And the holy dove was moving too
And every breath we drew was Hallelujah

Verse 6:
Maybe there's a God above,
But all I've ever learned from love
Was how to shoot somebody who out drew ya.
And it's not a cry that you hear at night,
It's not somebody who's seen the light,
It's a cold and it's a broken Hallelujah.

No Woman, No Cry

Words & Music by Vincent Ford

Arpeggio style:

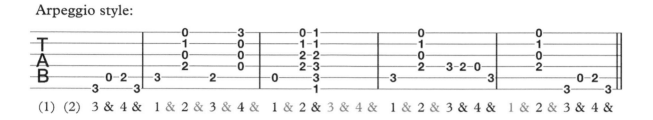

Accompaniment: 4/4 Rhythm

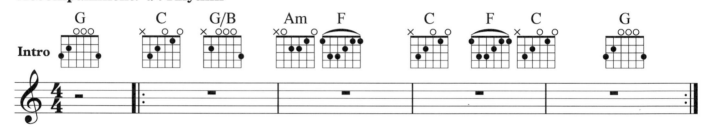

No wo-man, no cry.

No wo-man, no cry.

No wo-man, no cry.

No wo-man, no cry.

No wo-man, no cry.

Here___ lit-tle dar-lin', don't shed no tears.

No wo-man, no cry.

No wo-man, no cry.

Said, said,

Said, said,

Verse

said I re-mem-ber when we used to sit in the gov-ern-ment yard in
said I re-mem-ber when we used to sit in the gov-ern-ment yard in

Trench-town. 1. O-ba, o-b-serv-ing the hyp-o-crites as they would
Trench-town. 2. 3. And then Geor-gie would make a fi-re-light as it was

min-gle with the good peo-ple we meet.
log wood burn-in' through the night.

Good friends we had, oh, good friends we've lost
Then we would cook corn meal por-ridge

a-long the way.
of which I'll share with you.

In this bright fu-ture you can't for-get your past
My feet is my on-ly car-riage,

11

Lyrics under the music:

so, dry your tears_____ I_____ say. And
so, I've got to push on_____ through, but while I'm gone I mean...

Middle

Ev-'ry-thing's gon-na be al-right. Ev - ry-thing's gon-na be al - right.

1.

Ev-'ry-thing's gon-na be al-right. Ev-'ry-thing's gon-na be al-right.

2.

Ev-'ry-thing's gon-na be al-right so, wo-man, no cry. No, no

wo - man, no wo - man, no cry. Oh, my lit-tle sis-ter,

don't shed no tears._____ No wo - man, no cry.

12

Suzanne

Words & Music by Leonard Cohen

Arpeggio styles:

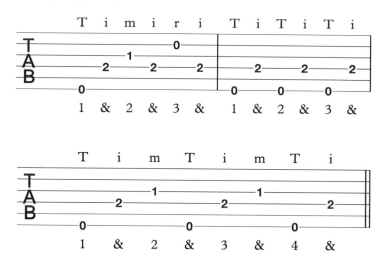

This song has bars of 3/4 *and* 4/4. It pays to look ahead to see where the 3/4 bars are so you're not taken by surprise.

Accompaniment: 3/4 and 4/4 rhythms

___ her. And you know___ that she's half cra - zy, but that's___

tow - cr. And when he knew for cert - ain, on - ly

count - ers. And the sun___ pours down like hon - ey on our

___ why you want to be there. And she feeds you tea and or -

drown - ing men could see him he said 'All men will be

la - dy of the har - bour. And she shows you where to

- ang - es that come all_____ the way from Chi - na. And just

sail - ors then un - til the sea shall free them'. But

look am - ong the___ gar - bage and the flow - ers there are

when you mean to tell her that you have no love to

he him - self was bro - ken long be - fore the sky would

her - oes in the sea - weed, there are chil - dren in the

give her, then she gets you on her wave - length, and she

op - en, for - sak - en al - most hum - an he

morn - ing, they are lean - ing out for love and they will

lets the riv - er an - swer that you've al - ways been her lov - er.
sank be - neath your wis - dom like a stone.
lean their way for - ev - er while Su - zanne holds the mir - ror.

And you want to tra - vel with her, and you
And you want to tra - vel with him, and you
And you want to tra - vel with her, and you

want to tra - vel blind._____ And you know she will trust_
want to tra - vel blind._____ And you think may - be you'll trust
want to tra - vel blind._____ And you know that you can trust_

_____ you, for you've touched her per - fect bod - y with your mind.
him, for he's touched your per - fect bod - y with his mind.
_____ her, for she's touched your per - fect bod - y with her mind.

1, 2.

3.

2. And

3. Now Su -

Duncan

Words & Music by Paul Simon

Arpeggio style:

The thumb will pick the bass note of the chord each time; the picking fingers can be placed on any three adjacent strings above the bass.

Accompaniment: 4/4 Rhythm
Capo: Fret 5

Intro   Bm   Verse Bm

1. Cou-ple in the next_____ room
3. Holes in my con - fi-dence,
5. Just la-ter on the ve-ry same night when I

A   D   E

bound to win a prize,_____ they've been go-in' at it all_____ night_____
holes in the knees of my jeans, I's left with-out_____ a pen - ny in my
crept to her tent with a flash - light,_ and my long years of in - no-cence

A   G   D

long, well, I'm tryin' to get some sleep, but these
pock - et. Oo hoo hoo_____ wee,_____ I's a-bout
end - ed,_____ well, she took me to_____ the woods, say - in',

17

mo - tel walls are cheap, Lin - coln Dun-can is___ my name and here's my
des - ti - tut - ed as a kid coud be,__ and I wished I wore a ring so I could
"Here comes some - thin' and it feels so good!" And just like a dog__ I was be -

song,_____ here's my song.
hock it,_____ I'd like to hock it.
- friend - ed,_____ I was be - friend - ed.   4. A

Verse

2.   My fa - ther was a fish - er - man, my ma - ma was a fish - er - man's friend,   and
(4.) young girl in a park - ing lot___ was preach - ing to a crowd, sing - in'
6. Oh, oh,_____ what a night, oh, what a gar - den of de - light, Ev - en

I was born in the bore - dom and the chow - der, so
sa - cred songs and read - ing from the Bi - ble, well, I
now that sweet me - mo - ry lin - gers, I was

when I reached my prime, I left my home in the Mar - i - times,_
told her I__ was lost, and she told me all__ a - bout the Pen - te - cost,__ and I
play - in' my gui - tar,__ ly - ing un - der - neath the stars,__ just

18

head-ed down the turn-pike for New Eng-land,____ sweet New Eng-land.
seen that girl as the road to my sur - vi - - - - val.
thank - in' the Lord for my fin - gers,____ for my fin - gers.

Interlude

1, 2. **3.**

Flutes

Outro

Repeat and fade

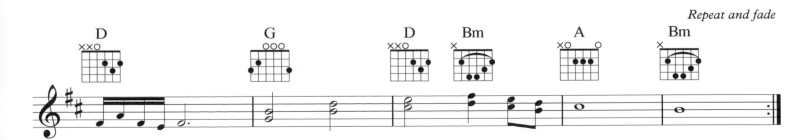

California Dreamin'

Words & Music by John Phillips & Michelle Gilliam

21

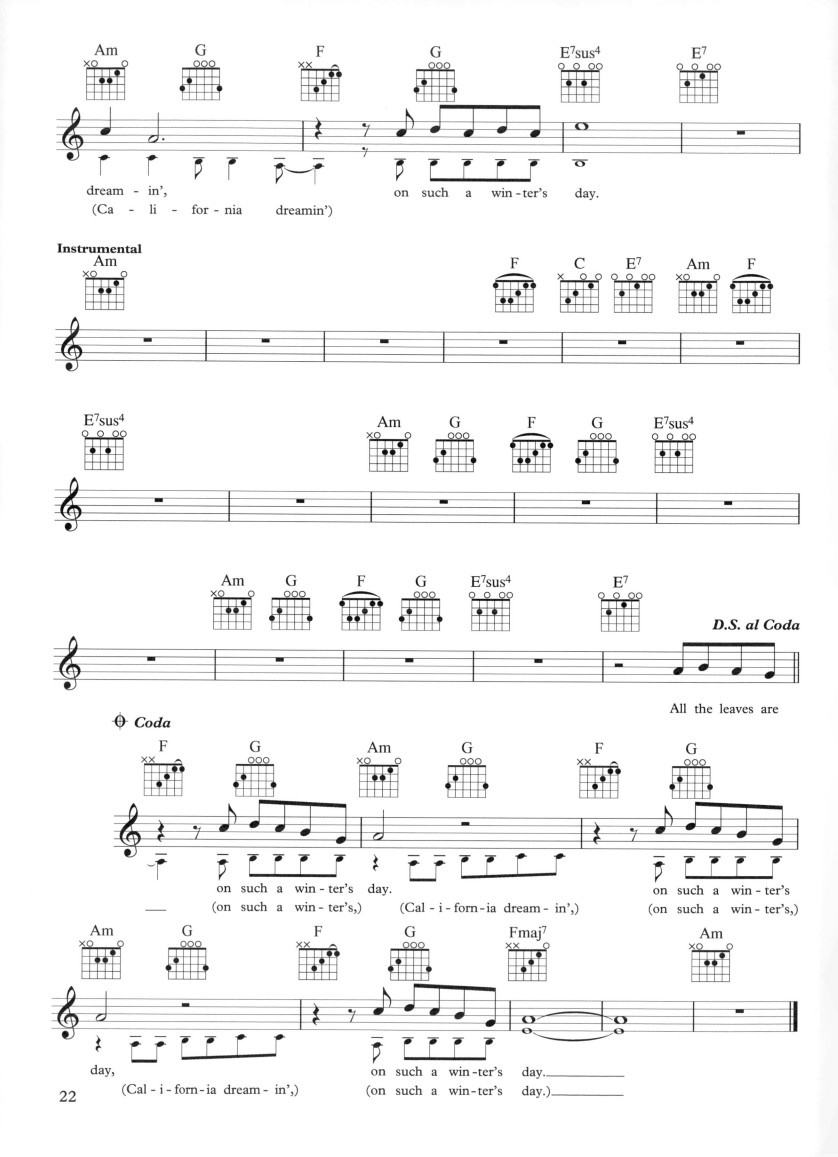

Don't Think Twice, It's All Right

Words & Music by Bob Dylan

Arpeggio style:

Accompaniment: 4/4 Rhythm
Capo: Fret 2

> Here's another candidate for memorising the chord sequence so you can concentrate on picking.

(1.) ain't   no   use   to   sit   and   won - der   why,_____   babe,
(2.)   no   use   in   turn - ing   on   your   light,_____   babe,
(3.) ain't   no   use   in   call - ing   out   my   name_____   girl,

4.   *(See block lyrics)*
5. (𝄋) *Instrumental*

the   light   I_____   if - fen   you   don't   know_____   by   now._____
                                    like   you   ne - ver   done_____   be - fore._____   ne - ver   knowed.__

And it ain't no use to
And it ain't no use in
And it ain't no use in

sit and won - der why,_____ babe,
turn - ing on your light,_____ babe,
call - ing out my name_____ girl,

it - 'll nev - er do some - how._____
I'm on the dark side of the road.
I can't hear you a - ny more._____

When your roost-
But I
I'm a-

- er_____ crows at the break_____ of dawn,_
wish there was some - thing you would_____ do or say,_
think - ing and a - wond - 'ring,_____ walk - ing down the road,_

look out_____ your win - dow and_____ I'll_____ be gone.
to try and make me change my
I once loved a wo - man, a child I am told._

You're the_____ rea - son I'm_____ a -
mind and stay. But we ne - ver did too much
I gave her my heart but she

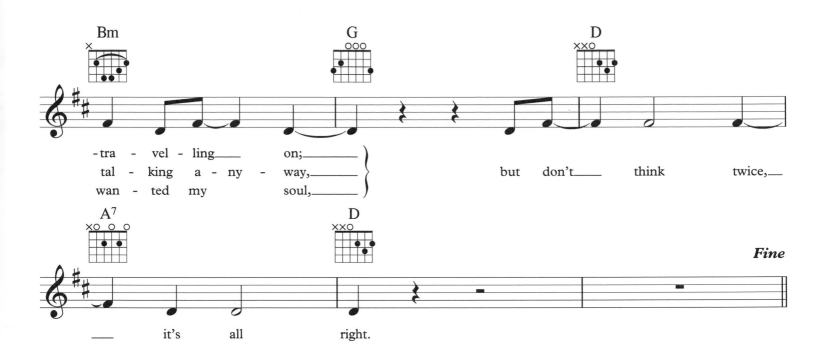

-tra - vel - ling_____ on;_____
tal - king a - ny - way,_____
wan - ted my soul,_____

but don't_____ think twice,_____

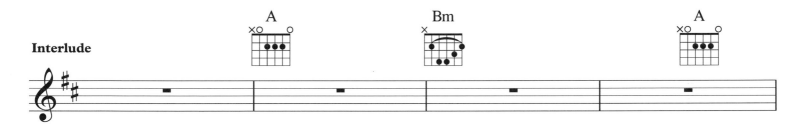

Fine

_____ it's all right.

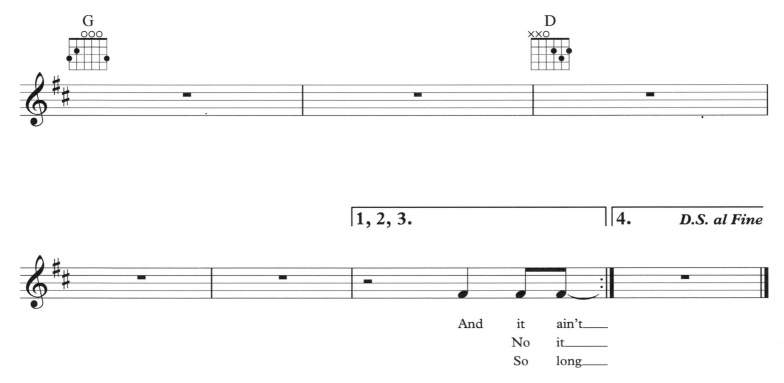

Interlude

1, 2, 3.

4. *D.S. al Fine*

And it ain't_____
No it_____
So long_____

Verse 4:
So long, honey babe
Where I'm bound, I can't tell
But goodbye's too good a word, babe
So I'll just say "Fare thee well"
I ain't saying you treated me unkind
You could have done better, but I don't mind
You just kinda wasted my precious time
But don't think twice, it's all right.

Imagine

Words & Music by John Lennon

Arpeggio style:

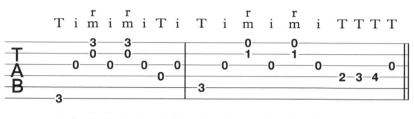

Accompaniment: 4/4 Rhythm
Capo: Fret 5

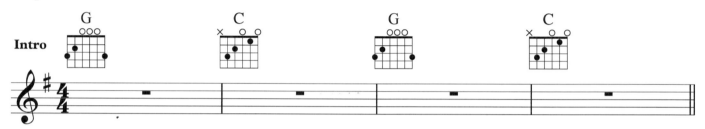

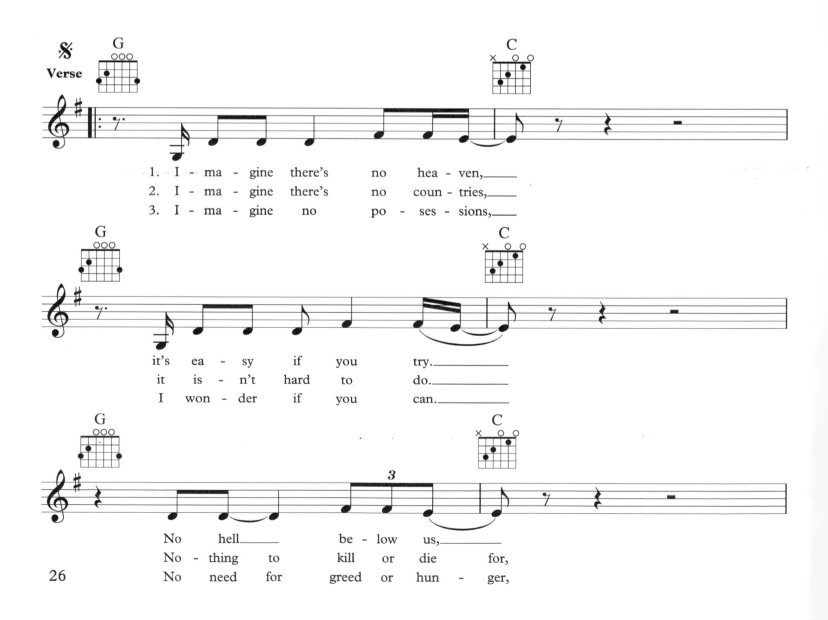

Live Forever

Words & Music by Noel Gallagher

Strumming style:

Practise strumming evenly and regularly, perhaps at a slower tempo first. It'll be worth it!

Accompaniment: 4/4 Rhythm

(1. 2. 4.) May - be___ I don't real - ly want to know how your gar-
(Verse 3 Instrumental)

- den grows I___ just want to fly___ Late - ly___ Did you

ev - er feel the pain in the morn - ing rain as it soaks___ you to the bone?___

Verse

(1. 4.) May - be I___ just want to fly, I want to live,___ I don't want to
(2.) May - be I___ will ne - ver be___ All the things___ that I want to

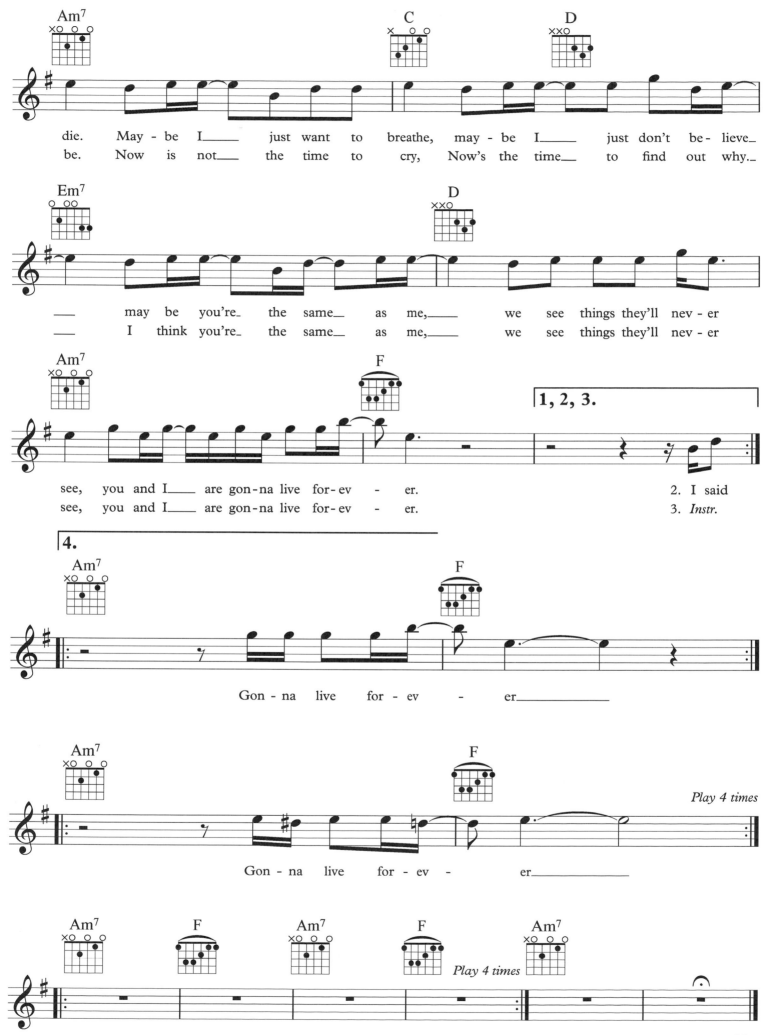

die. May - be I____ just want to breathe, may - be I____ just don't be - lieve
be. Now is not____ the time to cry, Now's the time____ to find out why.__

____ may be you're_ the same_ as me,____ we see things they'll nev - er
____ I think you're_ the same_ as me,____ we see things they'll nev - er

1, 2, 3.

see, you and I____ are gon-na live for-ev - er.
see, you and I____ are gon-na live for-ev - er.

2. I said
3. *Instr.*

4.

Gon - na live for - ev - er_____

Play 4 times

Gon - na live for - ev - er_____

Play 4 times

The 59th Street Bridge Song (Feelin' Groovy)

Words & Music by Paul Simon

> The intro section is quite long, but part of it is recycled for the verse: play bars 3 and 4 of the intro for the repeating two-bar verse sequence.

Arpeggio style:

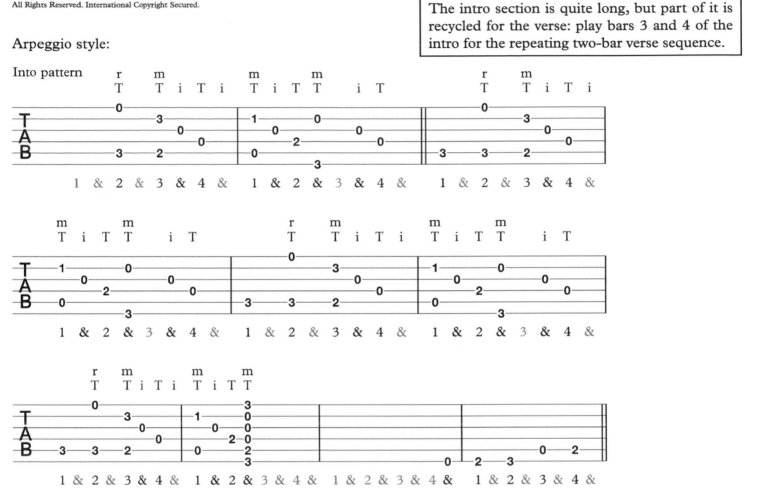

Into pattern

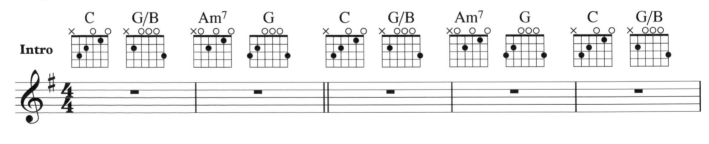

Accompaniment: 4/4 Rhythm (Swing)
Capo: Fret 3

Intro

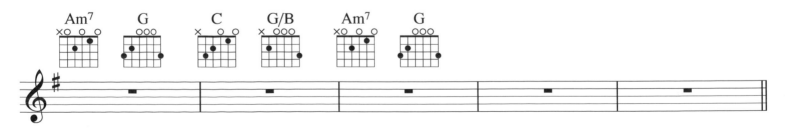

The Boxer

Words & Music by Paul Simon

Arpeggio style:

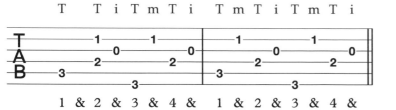

> A great feature of this song is the alternating bass notes below the picking pattern. Try it slowly at first until it's nice and smooth.

Accompaniment: 4/4 Rhythm

Tune down one semitone: E♭ A♭ D♭ G♭ B♭ E♭

1. I am just a poor boy. Though my sto - ry's sel - dom told, I have squan - dered my re - sis - tance for a pock - et - ful of mum - bles, such are pro - mi - ses.____

(2.) left my home and my fam - i - ly,___ I was no more than a boy in the com - pa - ny___ of stran - gers in the qui - et of a rail - way sta - tion run - ning scared,____

(3.) on - ly work - man's wag - es I come looking for a job, but I get no of - fers,____ just a come - on from the whores on Sev - enth Av - en - ue.____

4. *Instrumental*

5. *(See block lyric)*

Am   G

___   lie - la - lie_____   la   la   la   la   lie -

C

- la   la   la   la   lie._____

1.   **2.**

                              C

                     3. Ask - ing   4. And   I'm

Verse

C   C/B   Am

lay - ing   out   my   win - ter   clothes_ and   wish - ing   I   was   gone,___   go - ing

G   G^7

home   where the   New York   Cit - y   win - ters   are - n't

C   Em

bleed - ing   me,_____   lead - ing   me,_____

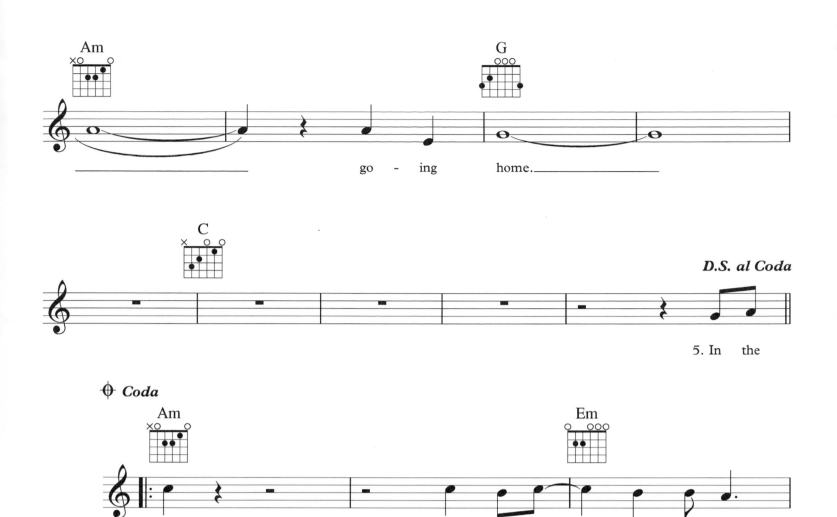

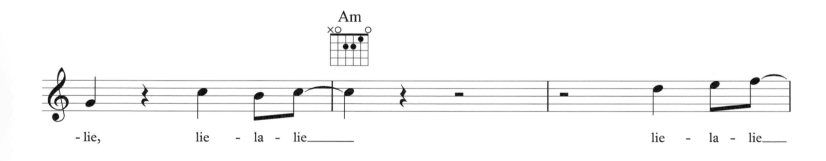

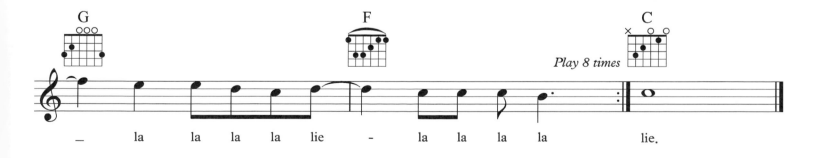

Verse 5:
In the clearing stands a boxer and a fighter by his trade
And he carries the reminders of every glove that laid him down
Or cut him 'til he cried out in his anger and his shame
"I am leaving, I am leaving" but the fighter still remains.

Can't Buy Me Love

Words & Music by John Lennon & Paul McCartney

Strumming style:

Pick the alternating bass notes firmly with the thumb, and work out which strings they'll be on ahead of time.

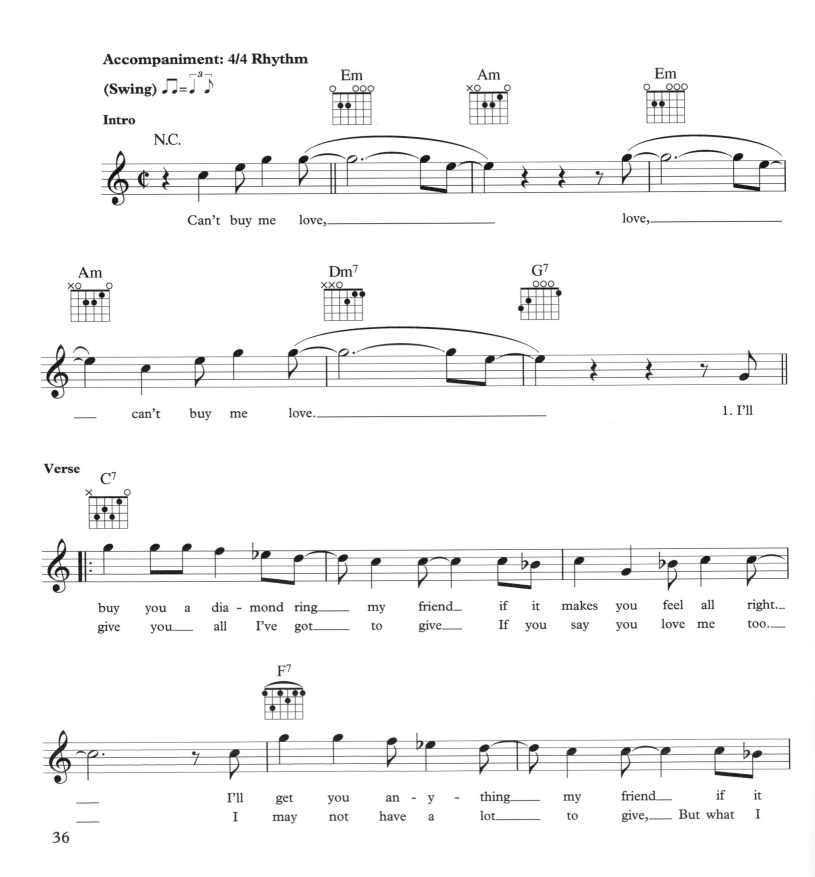

makes you feel all right.____ 'Cause I don't care too
got I'll give to you.____ I don't care too

1. **2.**

much for mo-ney, mo-ney can't buy me love.____ 2. I'll
much for mo-ney, mo-ney can't buy me love.__ ____ Can't buy me love,_

Chorus

____ ev-'ry-bo-dy tells me so.____ Can't buy me love,_

____ no no no____ no.

Verse

3. 4. Say you don't need no dia-mond rings,_ and I'll be sa-tis-fied.____ Tell_

____ me that you want the kind of things_ that mo-ney just__ can't buy.____ I__

37

don't care too much for mo-ney; mo-ney can't buy me love.

(Guitar solo)

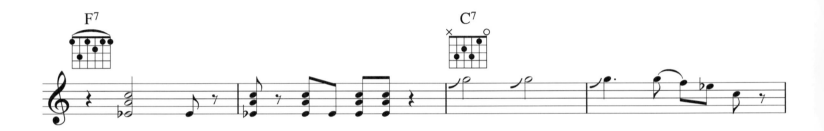

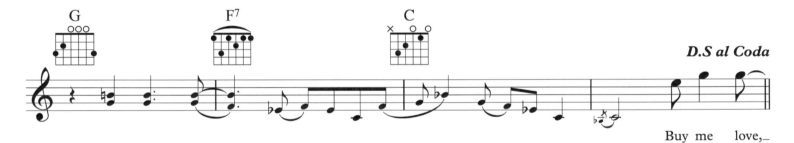

Buy me love,_

Coda

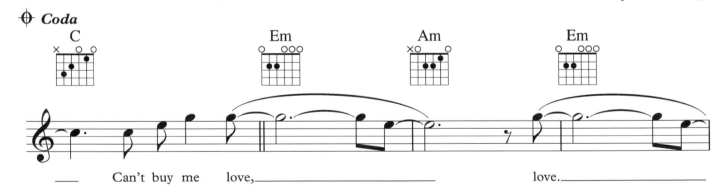

_Can't buy me love,_____ love._____

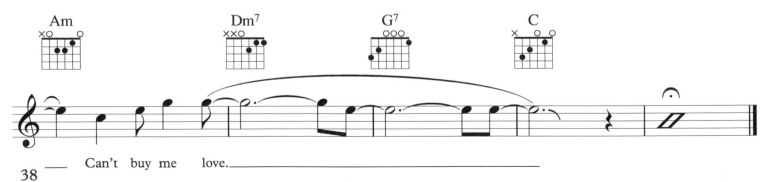

_Can't buy me love._____

38

Always On My Mind

Words & Music by Mark James, Wayne Thompson & Johnny Christopher

Arpeggio style:

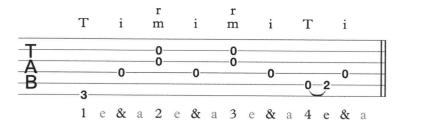

Accompaniment: 4/4 Rhythm

You were al - ways on my mind (You were al - ways on my

mind.) You were al - ways on my___ mind. | mind.

Tell___ me, tell me that your sweet love___ has-n't

died.___ Give___ me, give me

one more chance to keep you sa - tis - fied,___ sa -

- tis - fied.

Lit - tle things I should have said___ and done, I just nev - er took the

40

41

Songbird

Words & Music by Christine McVie

Arpeggio style:

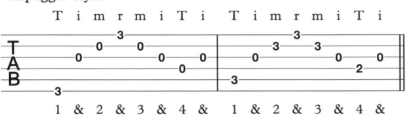

> Keep relaxed and let the picking pattern flow naturally, being sure to pick the correct bass note each time.

Accompaniment: 4/4 Rhythm

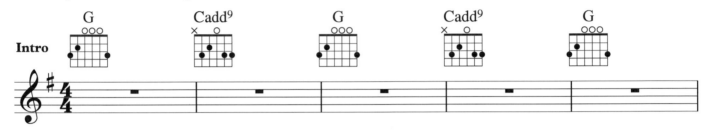

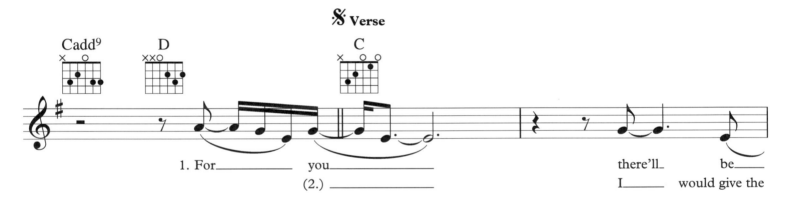

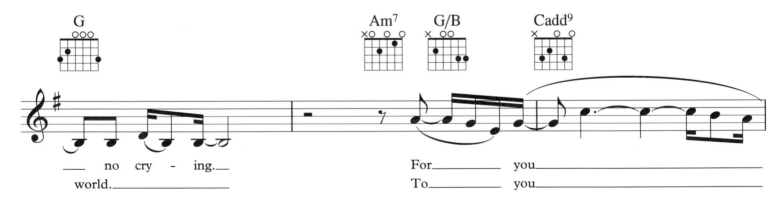

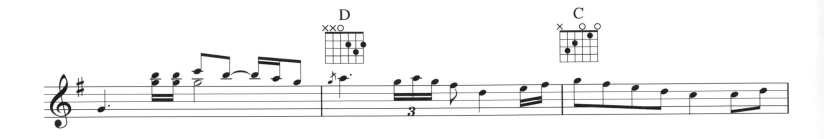

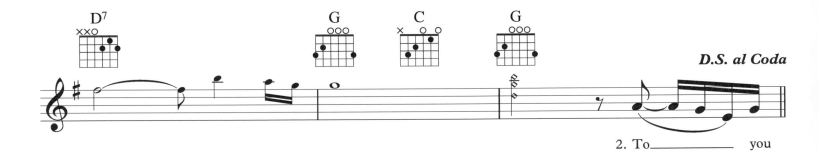

D.S. al Coda

2. To_____ you

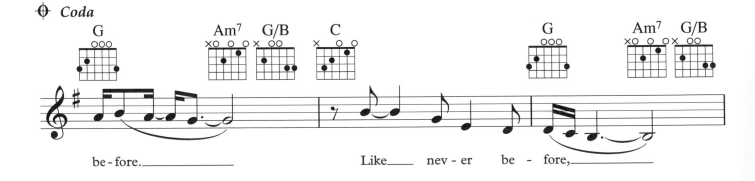

be - fore._____ Like____ nev - er be - fore,_____

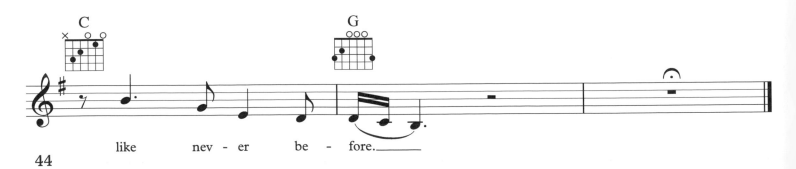

like nev - er be - fore._____

44

The Air That I Breathe

Words & Music by Albert Hammond & Mike Hazlewood

Strumming style:

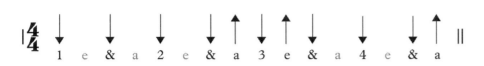

Accompaniment: 4/4 Rhythm
Capo: Fret 3

Intro

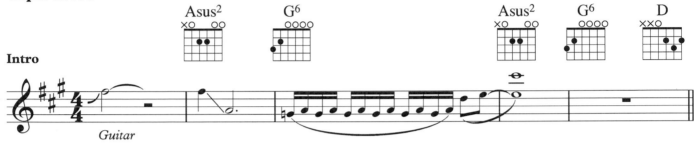

Verse

If_____ I could make___ a wish,___ I think_ I'd pass,____

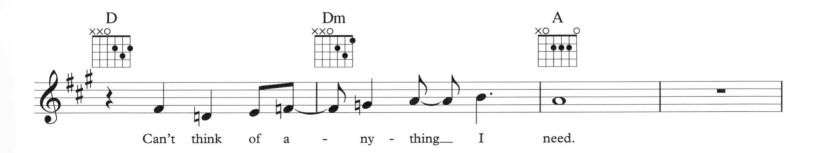

Can't think of a - ny - thing___ I need.

No____ ci - ga - rettes,___ no sleep,___ no light, no sound,___

No - thing to eat,___ no___ books to read. Mak - ing love with

you_____ has left me peace - ful, warm, and tired.___ What_____ more could I

ask? There's no - thing left_____ to be de - sired.

Pre chorus

Peace_____ came up - on___ me and___ it leaves_____ me weak.

So sleep, si - lent an - gel, go to sleep.

46

Chorus

Some - times,___ all I need is the air___ that I breathe and to love you.___

All I need is the air___ that I breathe, yes to love you.___ All I need is the air

___ that I breathe.___

1. Instrumental

2.

Some - times,___

Repeat to fade

all I need is the air___ that I breathe and to love___ you.

47

Norwegian Wood (This Bird Has Flown)

Words & Music by John Lennon & Paul McCartney

Strumming style:

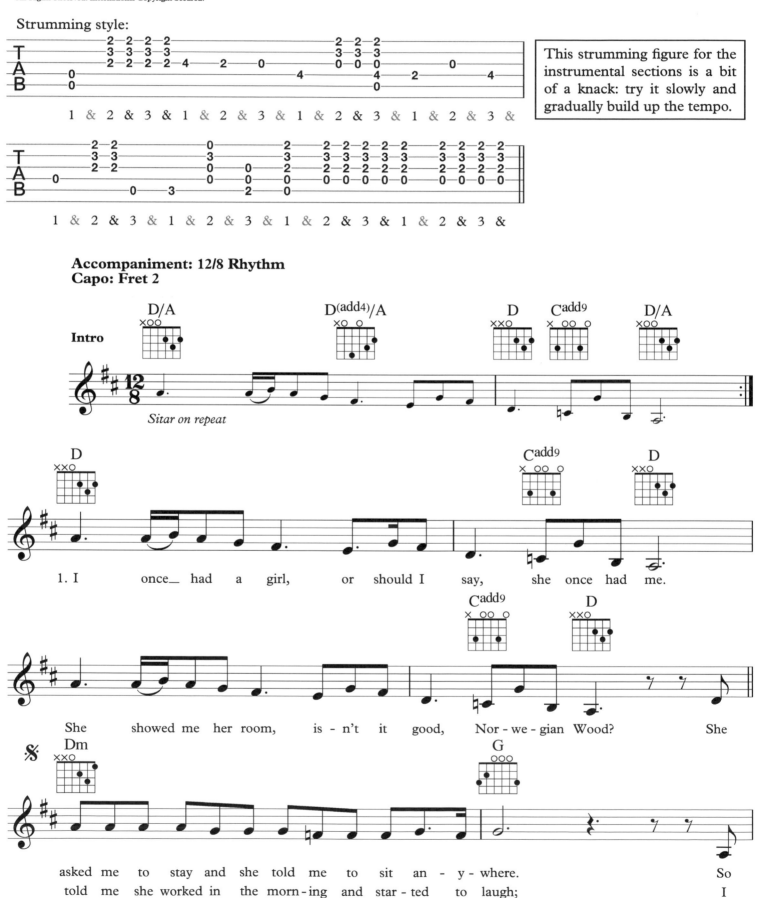

This strumming figure for the instrumental sections is a bit of a knack: try it slowly and gradually build up the tempo.

I looked a - round and I not - iced there was - n't a chair.
told her I did - n't and crawled off to sleep in the bath.

I sat on a rug, bid - ing my time, drink - ing her wine.
And when I a - woke I was a - lone, this bird had flown.

To Coda ⊕

We talked un - til two and then she said, "It's time for bed."
So, I lit a fire, is - n't it good, Nor - we - gian Wood?

D.S. al Coda

2. She

⊕ *Coda*

49

More Than Words

Words & Music by Nuno Bettencourt & Gary Cherone

Arpeggio style:
(Thumb picks lower notes; top three strings picked with 1st, 2nd & 3rd fingers).

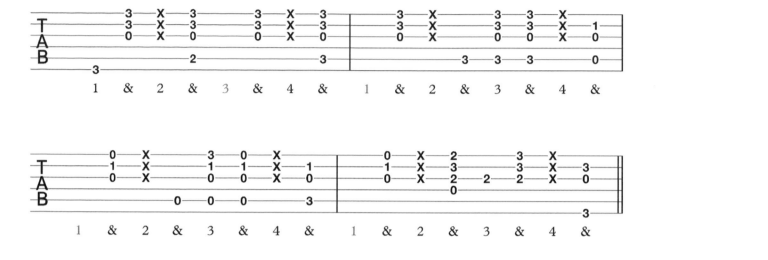

Accompaniment: 4/4 Rhythm

Tune 1 semitone down: E♭ A♭ D♭ G♭ B♭ E♭

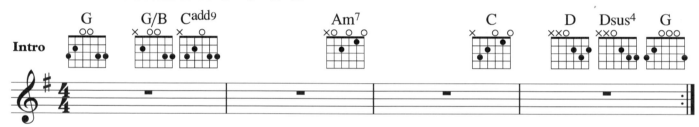

1. Say - ing "I____ love____ you," is not the words_ I want_
2. Now that I've____ tried____ to talk to you____ and make_

____ to____ hear from you,____ it's not that I____ want____ you,
____ you un - der - stand,____ All____ you____ have to do is

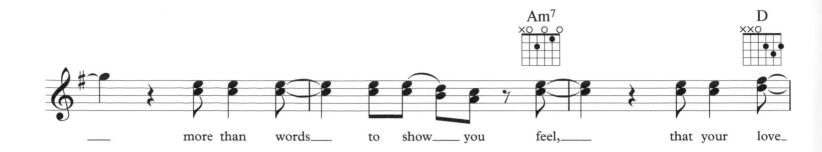

more than words___ to show___ you feel,___ that your love___

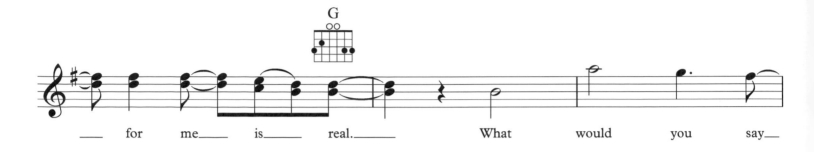

___ for me___ is___ real.___ What would you say___

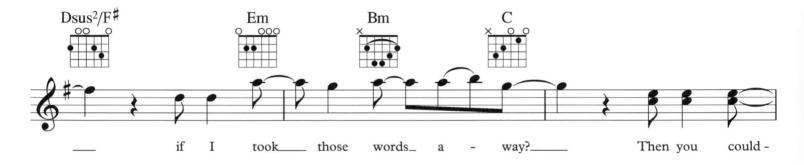

___ if I took___ those words_ a - way?___ Then you could -

- n't make___ things new,___ just by say - ing I___ love___ you.

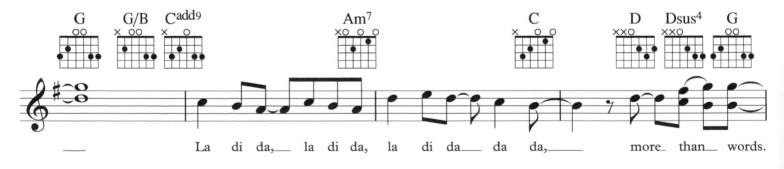

___ La di da,___ la di da, la di da__ da da,___ more_ than_ words.

1.

La di da,___ la di da.___

52 ___

Wonderwall

Words & Music by Noel Gallagher